# Windows on the Passion

# WINDOWS ON THE PASSION

Donald English

MATERIALS FOR GROWTH IN CHRISTIAN FAITH AND LIFE

P.O. Box 189 • Nashville, TN 37202 • Phone (615) 340-7285

Also of interest by Donald English
THE MEANING OF THE WARMED HEART

Unless otherwise noted, all scriptures quoted are from the Holy Bible, New International Version. Copyright © 1973, 1978, International Bible Society. Used by permission of Zondervan Bible Publishers.

Library of Congress Catalog Card No. 88-62508

ISBN 0-88177-066-3

An earlier brief version of this book was published in 1978 by Epworth Press, London, England.

WINDOWS ON THE PASSION. Copyright © 1988 by Donald English. All rights reserved. Printed in the United States of America. No part of this book may be reproduced in any manner whatsoever without written permission except in the case of brief quotations embodied in critical articles or reviews. For information address Discipleship Resources Editorial Offices, P. O. Box 840, Nashville, TN 37202.

DR066B

# Contents

One Story with Many Windows  *vii*

1. A Story Behind a Story  Matt. 24:29-31  1

    Written Sources  Mark 13:24-27  3
    Forms  Luke 21:25-28  4
    Historical Development  Luke 21:25-28  5

2. Understanding the Death of Jesus  2 Cor. 5:11-21  9

    A Proof  11
    A Sacrifice  11
    A Substitution  13
    A Victory  16

3. The Death of Jesus—Matthew  Matt. 27:45-56  19

    Matthew  20
    Old Testament Crossroads  20
    Old Testament Teacher  22
    An Old Testament King  24

4. The Death of Jesus—Mark          Mark 15:33-41      29

    Mark    30
    John the Baptist    31
    The Cross of Jesus    33
    Jesus the Carpenter    34

5. The Death of Jesus—Luke          Luke 23:44-49      39

    Luke    39
    Backdrop    40
    Rogues' Gallery    43

6. The Death of Jesus—John          John 19:28-37      49

    John    50
    Many Colors    50
    Earth Tones    54
    Believe and Receive    56

  Go Through Your Window    59

# ONE STORY WITH MANY WINDOWS

In Britain there are many buildings known as "stately homes." Similar homes are found in the eastern part of the United States. They are the large or very large houses in which the lords and ladies of bygone centuries lived, often in great luxury and with huge staffs of servants to care for them. The grounds were frequently landscaped in order to produce maximum good effect as visitors approached, not least if it was the ruling monarch.

Today the heirs of many of those families still occupy these homes, but in very different circumstances. The staff of the estate is greatly reduced in size and the stately home must be run economically. One solution is to open the homes to the public. On payment of an entry fee you can see Blenheim Palace, hereditary home of Winston Churchill's family, or Chatsworth House, or Woburn Abbey.

On one lovely spring day, all the better for being a day off, my wife and I decided to visit one of these stately homes. Unfortunately we omitted to discover one important piece of information. The day we chose to visit was the one day in the week that the house was closed to the public!

We were allowed into the grounds, however. So we saw all

that we could by peering through the ground-floor windows. Noses pressed against the glass, hands cupped to increase vision, necks craned to see as much as possible, we discovered the fascination of seeing the same room through various windows. Each viewpoint gave us a different perspective.

In a way, that is the advantage of having four Gospels telling the one story of Jesus Christ. Each Gospel writer is like a window, or a series of windows, onto the same room. As we look with their help, each window tells us particular things about Jesus Christ.

This is true of his Passion; that is, his suffering and death. The Passion takes up one-third of Matthew and Mark, a quarter of Luke, and half of John. The story itself is much the same in each, but the setting is different. For in each, the Passion of Jesus Christ is the culmination of certain parts of the story which the writer wishes to underline. It is like the stately home again. If you approach it by one route, you notice the landscaping. By another, you will be impressed by the gardens. By yet another, you are struck by the starkness of the house on the horizon. It is the same house, but a difference of approach gives a difference of perspective. So it is with the Gospels.

We benefit from the varied Gospel accounts of Christ's Passion if we know how to make the most of them. It is important to hold on to the fact that each writer has a purpose of his own. The way he describes the Passion of Jesus Christ will fit in with the way he tells the whole story, both in terms of the amount of the space he gives it and the details he includes. Alongside this coherence, however, there is also the question of why any one Gospel writer leaves out parts of the story which others include. It could be that he had not been given that information. It could be that he did not have the space available. Or it may simply be that those particular parts of the story were not wholly relevant to the point he was making. There is interest in the contrast.

Above all, however, our aim in reading each is to learn what we can about the meaning of the death of Jesus Christ, and, in particular, its meaning for our lives. The variety and the harmony of the four Gospel accounts will help us greatly to fulfill that aim.

# 1
# A STORY BEHIND A STORY

## THE PAROUSIA OF THE SON OF MAN
### (Revised Standard Version)

| Matt. 24:29-31 | Mark 13:24-27 | Luke 21:25-28 |
|---|---|---|
| 29 "Immediately after the tribulation of those days the sun will be darkened, and the moon will not give its light, and the stars will fall from heaven, | 24 "But in those days, after that tribulation, the sun will be darkened, and the moon will not give its light, 25 and the stars will be falling from heaven, | 25 "And there will be signs in sun and moon and stars, and upon the earth distress of nations in perplexity at the roaring of the sea and the waves, 26 men fainting with fear and with foreboding of what is coming on the world; |
| and the powers of the heavens will be shaken; 30 then will appear the sign of the Son of man in heaven, and then all the tribes of the earth will mourn, and they will see the Son of man coming on the clouds of heaven with power and great glory; 31 and he will send out his angels with a loud trumpet call, and they will gather his elect from the four winds, from one end of heaven to the other. | and the powers in the heavens will be shaken. 26 And then they will see the Son of man coming in clouds with great power and glory. 27 And then he will send out the angels, and gather his elect from the four winds, from the ends of the earth to the ends of heaven. | for the powers of the heavens will be shaken. 27 And then they will see the Son of man coming in a cloud with power and great glory. 28 Now when these things begin to take place, look up and raise your heads, because your redemption is drawing near." |

The story of how the New Testament Gospels came to be written is a fascinating one, though all the details are by no means known. The central question is how the gap between the ministry of Jesus and the written form of the Gospels was filled. That basic issue throws up a number of other questions. How strong were the memories of the people who heard Jesus? In a culture without diaries, computers, and other memory support systems, human memory needed to be relied upon for accuracy over a wider range of issues than is the case today. Did people rely only upon their memories? If not, how was material preserved? Did the Gospel writers use a wide range of such material? How reliable are the Gospels in the light of this process? Can we compare the relative reliability of the different ways in which the memories were preserved? Can we (and ought we to) compare the different Gospels for relative reliability in their accounts of Jesus? Probably the best response to such queries is a description of how biblical scholars have sought to deal with this area of understanding the Bible.

Before answering these questions, however, two points of clarification are necessary. First, to discuss the ways in which the material was preserved and passed on is not necessarily to question the presence of the Holy Spirit in the process. It is to discuss the method, not the degree of divine inspiration. Second, to discuss how any part of the Gospels came to be constructed is not to cast doubt on God's ability to inspire those who read the Bible today. The overall concern is how disciples of Jesus, under the guidance of the Holy Spirit, composed the Gospels; and how disciples of Jesus today,

# A Story Behind a Story

under the guidance of the same Holy Spirit, read and understand the Gospels.

## WRITTEN SOURCES

*How can we explain the gap between the ministry of Jesus and the writing of the Gospels?* (Estimates vary as to how long the gap was, but we should probably allow for at least a decade or two.) One approach has to do with written documents, though none of these original documents still exist. Look at the parallel layout above about the Parousia (Coming) of the Son of Man. By studying the Gospels in a comparative way, scholars discover places where two or three of the synoptic Gospels (Matthew, Mark, and Luke) agree exactly on precise wording. John is plainly different and later. *Synoptic* comes from a Greek word meaning "seen together." In some cases two would have identical wording but the third would differ. Each of the three has material not used by the others. These differences and agreements among the synoptic Gospels were solved by suggesting the existence of various original documents, identified by putting together the material from the Gospels where there was exact agreement, and singling out the passages where different writers were using different versions, or telling stories not found anywhere else. (Only Luke, for example, tells the story of the good Samaritan.) The diverse documents whose existence was posited were given names such as Q (from the German word *quelle,* meaning "source"), which Matthew and Luke used when adding to what they got from Mark's Gospel itself. They use L and M for the sections peculiar to Luke and Matthew respectively, and even the mysterious sounding Ur-Markus, an allegedly early form of some of Mark's material. Anyone can play the game for herself or himself by putting copies of the Gospels side by side (in a parallel) where they refer to similar events or speeches, and coloring with different colors the various areas of agreement and disagreement.

## FORMS

The second possibility, somewhat in reaction to looking at written sources, is a study of the forms of speech used in the Gospels. A study of written sources is felt to be too limiting, both in the distribution of the alleged documents and because it bore little direct relevance to the ongoing life of the growing church. By studying the forms, we see the Gospel material as preserved much nearer the heart of the Christian church than by the isolated writing of a few people. It locates the continuing memory in the preaching and teaching. It identifies different forms in which the material was preserved, such as miracle stories, pronouncement stories, and so on. It also allows for the life setting of the preaching and teaching, and tries to show how the context exerted its influence upon what was taught. Thus memorable statements such as "the first shall be last and the last, first" turn up attached to different contexts and stories.

## HISTORICAL DEVELOPMENT

A third approach looks at the alleged progress of the material as time went on, not least in relation to different cities or areas where particular emphases were said to be preserved, so that different regions offered varied insights into Gospel material. It also makes due distinction between what actually was the truth, and the artificial historical setting (called a myth) created to embody it.

The result of these and other approaches was to qualify an earlier view of the Gospels as telling history in the way we tell it, beginning at the beginning and going in strict historical order to the end. The Gospel writers, it was generally acknowledged, each have a point to make, and will order the material accordingly. This led to a fourth form of study, which concentrated heavily on how each Gospel writer shaped and ordered his accounts in order to make his particular point or reach his particular audience. This would account for the diversity of order in the Gospels, and for the fact that a well-known story or saying can come near the beginning of one and the end of another. It is not unhistorical: it is a different way of writing history. Interestingly enough, some modern historians are moving in a direction not too distant from this by their insistence on the partiality of the historian as he or she tells a story.

Of course, all of this study can be extremely threatening, especially as some scholars have used it. It can cast doubt on the accuracy of much of the Gospel material as a reliable account of what happened. It can suggest that Gospel writers invented a lot of the material and put it into the life and mouth of Jesus as a way of declaring what they believed to be true. It can see the Gospels, not as the account of what Jesus said and did, but as a record of what the early church believed at the time of writing. Any of these attitudes can change one's view of the inspiration and authority of the Bible.

Yet these approaches do not have to be used in that way. When they are thus used they reflect the views of the particular scholar, and are not absolutely required by the discipline being used. At base they are simply ways of answering our first question about how the gap between Jesus' ministry and the writing of the Gospels was filled, and how the material got from the one to the other. God is as capable of preserving the truth through one method as through another. The variety in the content of the Gospels means that we have a richer perspective than we would otherwise have had, as this little book seeks to show, looking through the different windows of the Gospel writers as they consider the death of Jesus Christ.

How are we to read the story of the Passion? We must first pray for the inspiration of God's Holy Spirit, that the One who inspired the writers will inspire the readers too. We must seek to find out all we can about the setting and the language of the first century. But we need also to read the Gospels through twentieth-century eyes, believing that they can speak to us today. I heard a missioner describe his task as enabling "the minuet between the text I wish to commend and the context in which I wish to commend it."

Through all the process we can trust God by the Spirit to teach us what we need to learn as we submit ourselves to God in reading the scriptures. Once we perceive something, we carry the added responsibility to live it out. Here, too, the Spirit enables us to do what God has inspired in us.

# 2
# UNDERSTANDING THE DEATH OF JESUS
## 2 Cor. 5:11-21

"Therefore, knowing the fear of the Lord, we persuade men; but what we are is known to God, and I hope it is known also to your conscience. We are not commending ourselves to you again but giving you cause to be proud of us, so that you may be able to answer those who pride themselves on a man's position and not on his heart. For if we are beside ourselves, it is for God; if we are in our right mind, it is for you. For the love of Christ controls us, because we are convinced that one has died for all; therefore all have died. And he died for all, that those who live might live no longer for themselves but for him who for their sake died and was raised.

From now on, therefore, we regard no one from a human point of view; even though we once regarded Christ from a human point of view, we regard him thus no longer. Therefore, if any one is in Christ, he is a new creation, the old has passed away, behold, the new has come. All this is from God, who through Christ reconciled us to himself and gave us the ministry of reconciliation; that is, in Christ God was reconciling the world to himself, not counting their trespasses against them, and entrusting to us the message of reconciliation. So we are ambassadors for Christ, God making his appeal through us. We beseech you on behalf of Christ, be reconciled to God. For our sake he made him to be sin who knew no sin, so that in him we might become the righteousness of God."

The importance which the earliest believers ascribed to the death of Jesus is shown by the large amount of space given to it in the Gospels. No other single event in the ministry of Jesus receives anything like the same amount of coverage. It is even possible to describe the accounts of his life as being primarily a preparation for his death, so important is it in the Gospels.

We shall see how that works out in the context of the Gospels themselves. As the events of Jesus' life are told in series, their significance for the particular writer, expressing the faith of the church, becomes clear. Successive chapters of this book will examine Christ's death in this way.

There is a different way of discovering the meaning of the Cross, however. It is to gather together the various references to it from right across the New Testament (read, of course, in the light of the Old Testament) to discover what the major emphases are in the Bible as a whole. These provide a context for looking at the various Gospel insights.

I am told that in Mozart's Jupiter Symphony there are five main themes which, in the end, are brought together in fugue in thirty bars. These thirty bars of music virtually combine fifteen themes. You do not need to know that to *enjoy* the music; but you do if you wish to *understand* it. It is the same with the death of Jesus. You can enjoy the forgiveness and peace it brings to those who believe, without searching into all the biblical explanations of it. But if you wish truly to understand what it means, you have somehow both to follow each section and to see how it all holds together.

## A PROOF

For example, the death of Jesus is seen as proof of God's love for us. Paul says in Romans, "But God demonstrates his own love for us in this: While we were still sinners, Christ died for us" (Romans 5:8). In a world where so many feel unloved, and where all of us from time to time recognize that we are unlovable, God has shown once for all in history that God loves us all. The proof is that Jesus has given his life for us. We may think that the world is often impersonal, or even that human qualities are decreasingly important. We may be tempted to despair about life because of the awful way in which we treat one another. But the Cross of Jesus Christ is planted in history as the supreme act of divine love to remind us that love is the secret of life in the world.

## A SACRIFICE

Christ's death is also seen in the New Testament as a sacrifice. In the Old Testament the people of Israel were given a sacrificial system by which to deal with their sinfulness. They knew that to do wrong broke the relationship with God which was so necessary to their well-being. The system by which they brought and offered sacrifices expressed certain deep theological convictions. First, God is holy love, and sin is not acceptable in God's world. Second, the person offering the sacrifice accepted personal responsibility and guilt for wrongdoing. Third, the sacrifice involved the sinner personally because one was bidden to take the best of the flock for offering, a thing no farmer would do with ease. In the fourth place, the making of sacrifices showed that a true relationship with God was a matter of life and death, and the Jewish understanding of "the life being in the blood" underlined this strongly.

It was with this background that the earliest Jewish Christians spoke of Christ's death as a sacrifice "once for all." The model of the "animal without blemish," used in their history now enabled them to see Jesus as the perfect offering for the sins of humanity. Just as the offerer of sacrifice in the Jewish system brought the best that he could, so, the argument ran, Jesus was offering a perfect life for all humanity, for all time and for every situation. You cannot get anything better than a perfect offering!

Yet the death of Jesus is not only different because it is humanly perfect. It is also different because God's involvement in the self-offering in Jesus was more than that envisaged in Old Testament sacrifice. God's part there was seen as being the originator of the system and the recipient of the sacrifice. The New Testament Christians saw God's involvement in the death of Jesus as much deeper than that. They saw God as being incarnate, "become flesh," in Jesus. "The Word became flesh and made his dwelling among us," John wrote (1:14). "For in Christ all the fullness of the Deity lives in bodily form," Paul writes of Jesus. They saw Christ as wholly man and wholly God. The death of Jesus not only involves humanity in a perfect offering for sin, therefore; it was God's perfect offering, too. All the other characteristics of Old Testament sacrifice are also present. Sin is accepted as an offense against a God of holy love. Responsibility for sin is accepted by the sinner. It is a matter of life and death that we should be right with God. God has provided a way in which we can be right. In penitence we accept God's provision for us, and by faith live a new life of forgiveness and love. It was in that spirit that the hymn writer affirmed that:

> There was no other good enough
> To pay the price of sin;
> He only could unlock the gate
> Of heaven and let us in.

(*Book of Hymns,* No. 414)

The cultural and religious models involved, such as animal sacrifice, may not be immediately congenial to us, but the realities which lie behind them are deeply familiar.

## A SUBSTITUTION

A third scenario for understanding Christ's death is provided by the difficult idea of "substitution." A great deal has been made of, and much theological consideration has been given to, the model of Jesus standing in for us.

> In my place, condemned, he stood,
> Sealed my pardon with his blood

wrote the hymn writer. For some persons that is not only unacceptable but the idea of someone else taking my punishment may even seem immoral. Much depends on whether we do justice to the teaching of the New Testament writers on the subject.

There can be little doubt that substitutionary atonement is part of New Testament understanding and proclamation. Jesus is seen to be more than simply our representative. He is that, as in Paul's words, "For as in Adam all die, so in Christ all will be made alive" (1 Corinthians 15:22). But Jesus is more. Paul says unequivocally that "God made him who had no sin to be sin for us, so that in him we might become the righteousness of God" (2 Corinthians 5:21). There is no escaping, in Old and New Testaments, this idea of the one offered *in place of* others.

We naturally react against such ideas. The thought of someone, especially someone wholly innocent, taking the place of another person, who is guilty, makes a good romantic story in a novel, but can hardly be taken as a proper basis for human justice. It is easy to present the story of the Cross in a way which reinforces this injustice, and which may even encourage irresponsibility on the part of sinners.

Such an error stems from a failure to see and understand the whole biblical understanding of Christ's death. One needs a wider focus to see it adequately. In the first place, as we saw in the case of Old Testament sacrifice, the reason for approaching the Cross at all is our awareness of our sin-

# Understanding the Death of Jesus

fulness and need. Only as we accept the fact that we have done wrong before God, and that we are responsible for it, can we begin to make proper sense of what the death of Jesus is about. Our engagement with his dying for us can no longer be distant or casual. It is for him and us a matter of life and death. Second, we must pay attention to the nature of the response expected of us. Too often it is presented only in terms of a formula: "Believe that Jesus died for you and you will be saved." In fact the New Testament records Jesus as saying, *not* "believe in the Cross" but "take up (your) cross" (Mark 8:34). Paul does *not* exhort his readers to believe that Jesus died and was raised. He tells them that to be a Christian is to be buried with Christ and raised with him (Romans 6:4). Faith in the death of Jesus on our behalf is much more than intellectual assent and emotional gratitude. It involves recognizing that *God counts all who commit their lives to Christ as dead to all that Christ died to, and raised to everything that Christ was raised to.* This is a theological truth which we accept intellectually, feel emotionally, and commit ourselves to with our wills. Faith in Christ's death, for us, is to accept that we are meant to be dead with him, to all that is evil, undesirable, contrary to God's will for God's world. It is equally to accept that we are raised with Christ to be part of all that God is seeking to do in God's world, to be obedient disciples in God's kingdom. Having accepted it, we seek to live that way. Just as Christ died and rose in our place to make eternal salvation available to all who will commit themselves in repentance and trust, so we are called daily to die and rise in Christ's place on earth. This is the implication of Paul's word to the Corinthians, again from 2 Corinthians 5, "For

Christ's love compels us, because we are convinced that one died for all, and therefore all died. And he died for all, that those who live should no longer live for themselves but for him who died for them and was raised again" (14-15). In the setting of a relationship, substitutionary atonement is robbed of the accusation of immorality, for we are truly gathered into what he did for us. What is more, our being gathered into his dying and rising is a fundamental motif of the Christian life as described in the New Testament.

## A VICTORY

So far we have seen the death of Jesus as a demonstration of God's love, as a sacrifice for sin, as standing in our place so that we might be saved. It is also seen as a spiritual victory. In a variety of metaphors and images, the New Testament writers portray Christ's crucifixion as the crucial battle between good and evil in the world. It is not the first or the last of such battles, but it is far and away the most significant, giving meaning to all the rest. It has been likened to the battle of El Alemein in the Middle East during the Second World War. It was not the final battle, in that sector or in that war, but once it was won, ultimate victory was assured. So it is with the death of Jesus.

Jesus' death is therefore portrayed in the New Testament as the event which opens up the holiest place to all who will approach (Hebrews 10:19-21); as the cancelling of debts against those who have sinned (Colossians 2:13-14); as the emptying of threat from death and sin (Romans 8:31-39).

# Understanding the Death of Jesus

Those who put their trust in the crucified (and risen) Christ, can enter into that victory for themselves as Christ dwells in them.

These varied ways of looking at Christ's death—as love, sacrifice, substitute, and victory—are all needed for a full and rounded view of what it means. They do not "make the music," any more than understanding about Mozart's Jupiter Symphony actually makes the music. The music is heard only as we live life based on the dying and rising of Christ. We will be helped to do that as we read the accounts of the Passion in the Gospels, looking through the various windows provided for us by the four Gospel writers.

Eph 2: 14-16

# 3
# THE DEATH OF JESUS
## Matt. 27:45-56

"From the sixth hour until the ninth hour darkness came over all the land. About the ninth hour Jesus cried out in a loud voice, 'Eloi, Eloi, lama sabachthani?' which means, 'My God, my God, why have you forsaken me?'

When some of those standing there heard this, they said, 'He's calling Elijah.'

Immediately one of them ran and got a sponge. He filled it with wine vinegar, put it on a stick, and offered it to Jesus to drink. But the rest said, 'Now leave him alone. Let's see if Elijah comes to save him.'

And when Jesus had cried out again in a loud voice, he gave up his spirit.

At that moment the curtain of the temple was torn in two from top to bottom. The earth shook and the rocks split. The tombs broke open and the bodies of many holy people who had died were raised to life. They came out of the tombs, and after Jesus' resurrection they went into the holy city and appeared to many people.

When the centurion and those with him who were guarding Jesus saw the earthquake and all that had happened, they were terrified, and exclaimed, 'Surely he was the Son of God!'

Many women were there, watching from a distance. They had followed Jesus from Galilee to care for his needs. Among them were Mary Magdalene, Mary the mother of James and Joses, and the mother of Zebedee's sons."

## MATTHEW

Many of us have watched international athletics on television. Quite apart from the events themselves, there is the tension which builds up just before an event takes place. The ways in which athletes focus their concentration is particularly fascinating. Nowhere is this truer than in relation to events which include a running start—long jump, high jump, and pole vault, for example. The athletes spend precious minutes getting themselves ready for the run. They know that if the run is wrong, the jump is hardly likely to be right.

Matthew's Gospel is, of all four, most concerned with the running start. Matthew seems to have a Jewish readership in mind. The Old Testament figures highly in his account. The way in which Christians can properly be God's chosen people, if that is what the Jews were, is a serious question he has to face.

## OLD TESTAMENT CROSSROADS

One of his roads to the Cross therefore starts far back in the Old Testament. He feels he must quote from it wherever

## The Death of Jesus—Matthew

possible to show that the story of Jesus as he tells it is really a fulfillment of what the Old Testament had already promised. So when Jesus is born, we are told "All this took place to fulfill what the Lord had said through the prophet: 'The virgin will be with child and will give birth to a son and they will call him Immanuel'—which means, 'God with us'" (1:22-23). John the Baptist's ministry is seen as fulfilling a prophecy of Isaiah. Jesus' triumphal entry into Jerusalem fulfills what Zechariah the prophet foretold, "Say to the Daughter of Zion, 'See, your king comes to you, gentle and riding on a donkey, on a colt, the foal of a donkey'" (21:5). Again and again he follows the road from Old Testament promise to New Testament fulfillment through Jesus Christ.

Why does Matthew do this? He wants us to know that it took a long time to prepare for the birth of Jesus. He did not come like a Martian out of the blue, with no human links with our world. His roots are firmly embedded in the history of the Jews. We take care to prepare for the coming of a baby today: God, says Matthew, took hundreds of years to prepare for the birth of Jesus.

But why is this point important for Matthew? Which window on the Passion is made accessible along this road? It is that God was at work in the history of his people the Jews, preparing the way for the coming of Christ, the Messiah. He wishes his readers to see that the one who suffers and dies is not just another Jew. He is the one in whom the whole of Jewish history is summed up, the deliverer whom they were seeking.

To a people whose religion treasured the presence of God he presents Jesus as "Immanuel, God with us." Readers who were proud of God's Law, given to them through Moses, now read the words of Jesus, "You have heard that it was said to the people long ago . . . but I tell you . . . " (e.g., 5:21-22). Those who are inclined to discount his importance hear him quote their own scriptures, "The stone the builders rejected has become the capstone; the Lord has done this, and it is marvelous in our eyes" (21:42). At every point Jesus is seen as the fulfillment of the best of Jewish faith and religion. It is as though all roads lead to one crossroads and he stands there as the common destination of them all.

A high point of this fulfillment is the Passion story. The Last Supper which Jesus shared with his disciples is full of Old Testament images, both in the form of the meal itself and in Jesus' reference to the Covenant. But at its heart is the offer of forgiveness of sins through the death of Christ. "This is my blood of the covenant, which is poured out for many for the forgiveness of sins" (26:28). He not only fulfills all the Old Testament promises, he gives his life to open the way for all persons to come to God. There is a cross at the crossroads where all Old Testament roads meet.

## OLD TESTAMENT TEACHER

That is not the only road by which Matthew leads to the Passion. He also lays emphasis on Jesus as teacher. It is Matthew who likes to gather the parables of Jesus into groups, so that in one chapter (Matthew 13) you find the sower, the wheat and the weeds, the mustard seed, the leaven, the hidden treasure, the pearl, and the dragnet. And it is Matthew who gives the Sermon on the Mount in its fullest form (Matthew 5-7).

Jesus' action in the Sermon on the Mount provides this window on the Passion. Put simply, Jesus is shown looking behind the Jewish Law in order to reveal the nature of the God who gave it. So he takes, as examples, some of the rules by which his fellow Jews lived—rules about murder and adultery, divorce and revenge. He not only repeats these, however, he also uncovers beneath them the inner attitudes which are more important to God. "You have heard that it was said, 'Do not commit adultery.' But I tell you that anyone who looks at a woman lustfully has already committed adultery with her in his heart" (5:27-28). One can almost hear the silence in response to that comment.

God, he is saying, is not primarily concerned with the rules you keep. God is more concerned with the kind of people you are. He goes to the sources of human life, and deals with the character and attitudes of a person, for these determine our words and deeds. And, at that level of our innermost being, he introduces the astounding command, "Be perfect, therefore, as your heavenly Father is perfect" (5:48). He uses the Law to reveal the nature of God, then shines it deep into the hearts of every one of us, searing out the deepest levels of our motives and attitudes, and then tells us to be like God. No wonder they were astounded!

The painful part was the turning of the mirror to face his hearers. They were not guilty of murder but had done their share of hating. They did not commit adultery, yet few felt free of lustful thoughts. They had offered their worship but their motives were not always the best. The pain was felt because what they saw of God in his teaching and what they saw of themselves were simply incompatible. They were poles apart.

Here is our second window on the Passion. As Jesus moves toward death on the Cross, he is embodying in himself the perfection of love and purity which is God's. But at the same time he has to bear upon himself the fury and rejection of those who could not bear to be shown how far from that perfection they themselves were. Yet he goes to the Cross for them, a person for persons, offering his perfect life to God on their and our behalf. He brings together, in himself, the life of God and the life of humanity in such a way that humanity is accepted. The death of Jesus assures me that no matter how far away I go from God, God's love is so great that I can, through Christ, live before God and not be afraid. I can both know the nature of God and live openly before God. Jesus Christ not only teaches the way of God, he is the way to God. The Law points the way to God; Jesus takes me to God.

# AN OLD TESTAMENT KING

A third road Matthew uses to bring us to a window on the Passion is marked out by the path Jesus himself takes in the Gospel story. In many ways it is the least promising road to take. Jesus at times seems determined not to be impressive. He appears to be easily trapped and executed by the authorities. He gives himself to the crowds and they desert him. He trusts his disciples and they fail him. From this angle it is a weary, disappointing road.

Yet it can be seen in a different light. Matthew manages to communicate to the reader that, unpromising though he often seems to be, Jesus is in fact on a royal progress along this road. He is not being hounded anywhere; he is himself picking his way.

Looked at from this point of view the story reveals another side to Jesus. At his birth Jesus is given gold—a kingly gift (2:11). He is described as the son of David (1:1), Israel's greatest king. In the Transfiguration (17:1-8) he is shown to be superior to Moses and Elijah. Before Pilate he acknowledges the title king of the Jews (27:11). Finally, he claims all authority in heaven and on earth (28:18). He commands disciples to follow him and they do so (4:18-22). He even sees himself as the central figure in the final Judgment. "Many will say to me on that day, 'Lord, Lord, did we not prophesy in your name, and in your name drive out demons and perform many miracles?' Then I will tell them plainly, 'I never knew you. Away from me, you evildoers!'" (7:22-23).

It is difficult to avoid the conclusion along this road that Jesus not only teaches about the kingdom of God, but that in some strange way he is the kingdom. Certainly, belonging to it seems to depend upon being in a right relationship with Jesus.

Here is our third window on the Passion. The kingdom of God is God's rule in the lives of persons. Jesus exemplifies this rule by his total obedience to the will of his Father.

He goes through his Passion making difficult choices, and always doing the will of God. The prayer in the garden of Gethsemane, "My Father, if it is possible, may this cup be taken from me. Yet not as I will, but as you will" (26:39), sums it up perfectly. And as that way of obedience leads him to the Cross, he dies so that all who wish may enter into the kingdom with him by submission to God's kingly rule.

Three windows on the Passion—all from Matthew. As we try to reflect upon the meaning of what God has done in Christ, Matthew offers these three directions for thought, three windows for our vision. Jesus Christ is the clue to God's activity in history, where all roads meet. He is the teacher who reveals the nature of God and yet also makes it possible to live before him openly. He is the one who not only proclaims the kingdom but actually embodies it, bringing with him all who will come.

But windows provide vision out as well as in. We search the Gospel story from our vantage point: the Gospel story searches us through the same windows. The roads by which we approach the windows are roads along which our discipleship can be worked out. We are invited again to press our noses to the glass, to shelter our eyes and crane our necks to gain the maximum view of Jesus as Matthew portrays him.

At the beginning of the Gospel we face the question, asked by the Wise Men, "Where is the one who has been born king of the Jews?" (2:2). At the end of the Gospel we are faced by a statement, this time from Jesus, "All authority in heaven and on earth has been given to me" (28:18). We can be grateful for all the perspectives on that which are given to us by Matthew.

# The Death of Jesus—Matthew

## A Prayer:

Father, we thank you that through the Passion of Christ we not only know you better, but also know ourselves better. Help us to submit our lives more fully to the love that you show us in Christ. Amen.

## Passages for Further Study in Matthew:

4:18-22
5:1–7:29
17:1-7

## Questions for Consideration:

a) How important is the Old Testament for our understanding of the New Testament?
b) How would you explain, in your own words, what Matthew tells us about the death of Jesus?
c) To which groups or types of person do you think Matthew's understanding of the Cross would be particularly relevant today?

# 4
# THE DEATH OF JESUS
## Mark 15:33-41

"At the sixth hour darkness came over the whole land until the ninth hour. And at the ninth hour Jesus cried out in a loud voice, 'Eloi, Eloi, lama sabachthani?'—which means 'My God, my God, why have you forsaken me?'

When some of those standing near heard this, they said, 'Listen, he's calling Elijah.'

One man ran, filled a sponge with wine vinegar, put it on a stick, and offered it to Jesus to drink. 'Now leave him alone. Let's see if Elijah comes to take him down,' he said.

With a loud cry, Jesus breathed his last.

The curtain of the temple was torn in two from top to bottom. And when the centurion, who stood there in front of Jesus, heard his cry and saw how he died, he said, 'Surely this man was the Son of God!'

Some women were watching from a distance. Among them were Mary Magdalene, Mary the mother of James the younger and of Joses, and Salome. In Galilee these women had followed him and cared for his needs. Many other women who had come up with him to Jerusalem were also there."

## MARK

History contains many accounts of the unjust deaths of good people—Abraham Lincoln, shot down in a theater; Archbishop Luwum, assassinated in Uganda; Mahatma Gandhi, murdered in India. The list goes on. In each case they were committed to causes widely regarded as true and just. Why did God allow them to die like that? Then there are those persons who are imprisoned because of their faith. Why should that happen to them if God is on their side? But why stop there with our questions? Why do any of us suffer in Christian discipleship? Surely God ought to take care of us better than it appears, if we are God's people.

In this book we are looking at the way in which each Gospel writer prepares the way for his description of the Passion of Jesus Christ. In the last chapter we looked through three of Matthew's windows. It was like approaching a house from a variety of directions and seeing different things through different windows. In this chapter we want to think about the windows in Mark's Gospel.

If Matthew led us to his windows along carefully laid paths, it is perhaps helpful to see Mark as leading us through particular people. After all, people can show you windows as easily as paths can lead you to them!

Take the people who first read Mark's Gospel, for example. They probably lived at the time of the Emperor Nero's persecution of Christians in Rome. This would account for the number of passages in the Gospel which refer to persecution; sayings about taking up one's cross (8:34), being faithful amidst this adulterous and sinful generation (8:38), being divinely compensated for loss and persecution here on earth (10:29-30), forthcoming disasters as the beginning of the sufferings (13:8), and about the need to bear witness in courtrooms and under interrogation (13:9-13). In other words, we are probably reading a Gospel written for Christians undergoing persecution, and about to go through a great deal more. The likely recent martyrdom of the Apostle Peter who, it is thought, provided Mark with much of his material, would heighten the feeling of danger among these Christians. Peter stands alongside the many others, some famous, a large number unknown, who have suffered for their faith. Their place in the story of the gospel is a normal one. They are not exceptions.

By thinking about the readers, however, whose names and characters we do not know, we are still too vague. We need more help than that in facing suffering and pain in our discipleship. We look for someone with whom we may identify, whose life and experience are clear enough and related enough to offer a comment on the problem we are considering. Is there anyone like that in Mark's story?

## JOHN THE BAPTIST

John the Baptist is one possibility. By contrast with Matthew and Luke, Mark shows little interest in his biography or in his preaching. Nor is there any account of conversation between John and Jesus. Yet John's ministry in the wilderness comes at the outset of Mark's Gospel. We read "the beginning of the gospel about Jesus Christ, the Son of God" (1:1) and then go straight into an account of John the Baptist. What is more, when John's death at the hands of King Herod is described later, Mark goes into great detail in telling the story and underlining the injustice of the execution (6:14-29).

But John the Baptist is not only the announcer of the story of Jesus (R.P. Martin, *Mark: Evangelist and Theologian*, Paternoster Press, 1972). John is also an example of what can happen to Jesus himself. John's presence in the Gospel, as Mark portrays it, is the first piece of shocking evidence that those who stand for what they know to be morally right are not necessarily greeted with acclaim, and especially if their lives and words are critical of those in authority. John the Baptist, in his integrity, had criticized the highest in the land (6:18). He now paid the price for living by the truth. Is Mark saying that the martyrs—those who suffer for their witness—are more than normal members of the Christian family? That they actually sum up in their experience what ought to be true of us all? I may not have my head offered on a platter to the king, or die by an assassin's bullet, or be a victim in a mass murder. But there are moments or experiences in our Christian discipleship which are different from these only in degree, and not in kind—moments when we pay the price for living by Christian standards, when we are murdered, not by bullets or knives but by the apathy of those who could not care less about the message of love which means so much to us; moments when we are unpopular for standing up to be counted in opposition to a general drift in the wrong direction. And if these experiences are of the same kind as those of the celebrated martyrs, ought I not to learn in some strange way to welcome them as signs of God's blessing rather than indication of God's neglect? John the Baptist died a ghastly death, without seeing the final fulfillment of the prophecies he had made. Yet his story is told wherever the message of Christianity goes. Looked at from this point of view, suffering for one's faith is not only normal and typical; it is a mark of true discipleship.

## THE CROSS OF JESUS

This brings us to the obvious person in Mark's Gospel to lead us to windows on the Passion—Jesus himself. The link with John is reinforced by a word Mark uses (in which he is copied by Matthew and Luke) to describe what happened to John and Jesus. It is a word variously translated "arrested," "betrayed," "delivered up," or "handed over." Its real significance lies in the fact that it is used in the Greek version of the Old Testament to refer to God's handing someone over, as in Isaiah 53:6 about the Suffering Servant. Literally translated, it reads, "The Lord delivered him for our sins." We are being invited to believe that in the case of John the Baptist, horrifying though his death was, even those events were not beyond the reach of God. Dare we believe that about our own suffering and hardship for the faith?

This dimension comes out very clearly in the picture Mark gives us of Jesus himself. One cannot help being impressed by the divine origin and character of this central figure of the Gospel, described at the outset as "Jesus Christ, the Son of God." Forty-seven percent of the first ten chapters is concerned with the miracles he performed; a theme which takes up, in all, 200 of Mark's 661 verses. He is the divine wonder-worker who heals the sick, casts out the demons, feeds the multitudes, and walks on the water—just the sort of hero a persecuted church would need, you might think. Or is he? Does such a person not merely frustrate us in our suffering? One with such powers could hardly enter into our exposure and weakness. And if Jesus is so powerful, why does he not deliver us now? If this is all Mark has to offer, perhaps Mark would have been better not to bother. Mark is facing us with the paradox of a strong leader with power to heal who nevertheless calls his people to suffer.

## JESUS THE CARPENTER

But if we look through another of Mark's windows, a whole new dimension opens up. The central figure of the story is described as the Son of God—but he is also spoken of as the carpenter. By using that image as the marker for our line of vision, we discover the other side of the story, an essentially human element. Jesus is moved with compassion, feels anger at the hardness of heart of his hearers, marvels at their unbelief, does not know the time of the end of the world, is greatly amazed and sorely troubled, and is finally humiliated by soldiers and crowds alike.

The help we seek in our troubles and difficulties is not dispensed for us by a superior, otherworldly being. Our strength is given by a person who has shared our humanity in its weakness and exposure, and knows the pain through which we go, for Jesus has been there before, and more

## The Death of Jesus—Mark

deeply than we have ourselves. Maybe in times of searing pain and loss this is the only source of comfort: he knows and understands and shares it with us. We are not alone; alongside us is one person whose suffering took human endurance to its deepest levels. He bore the pain and anguish of the sins of the world upon himself, and it is he who suffered at that depth who now shares our suffering with us. This knowledge may be, in some situations, the only source of comfort which we can feel to be meaningful. Others may not understand our pain and experience—Jesus does. Mark wants us to know that there is no human dereliction which Jesus cannot feel. When our prayers seem to go no higher than the ceiling, our cries for help seem of no avail, our suffering isolates us from everyone else, there is still one who stands there—also alone—and shares our suffering with us. In John's Gospel (19:30), Jesus utters a cry of victory from the Cross. In Luke (23:46), there is a prayer in which he commits himself to God the Father's care. In Matthew (27:51-54) unusual events declare that God is on his side. In Mark, there is total silence (R.P. Martin, *Mark: Evangelist and Theologian*).

But the disciples found it very difficult to accept the determination with which Jesus went to his death in Jerusalem. The crisis came for them at Caesarea Philippi (8:27-38). There Peter confessed him to be the Christ, God's chosen one, but was then rebuked when he tried to prevent Jesus from going to Jerusalem and death. They had to choose between a human way and God's way.

It was this confession of Jesus as the Christ which prepared the way for him to talk about the Cross, which had only been hinted at earlier in the Gospel. Once the disciples knew who he was, they could discover what he had come to do. His mission was not simply to give advice on how to live. He came to set people free from the power of evil, and in God's name to make a way to God for man and woman. He took the inevitable suffering involved in evil's battle with good, and turned it to positive, redemptive ends. His suffering became a source of good in the world.

Here we unlock the crucial window in Mark's Gospel. The window through which we look opens up to enable us to enter. We are invited to walk with Christ who calls his disciples each to take up his own cross and follow (8:34). We are not offered an easy way. To be engaged in the battle between good and evil in the world makes that impossible. The benefits of being a Christian are not the main reason for being one. We are called to discipleship because it is the true way to walk through life. And it is right as well as true. We may not understand the mystery of the presence of evil in the world. But we can know which side we are on. In Jesus Christ God has declared the wrongness of evil, the rightness of good, and called us to commitment in the struggle. We shall not follow Jesus' way without cost, but we can know that it is the way which love must take. And there is one inestimable benefit. Jesus walks with us, or in Mark's terms at the end of the Gospel, goes ahead of us (16:7). Our sufferings in his service are not meant to be lonely experiences; they can link us to the one who suffered the weight of human sin upon himself and carried it out of the way; his presence assures us that our suffering is neither out of God's care, nor purposeless. Jesus stills the storms, feeds the hungry, and speaks with authority. In bearing our pain we can know his presence—the greatest

# The Death of Jesus—Mark

gift of all. Even in suffering and hardship, he is still the good news.

## A Prayer

Help us, Lord, in our times of suffering and loneliness, to know the presence of Christ; and to find in that presence our comfort and hope; through Jesus Christ, our Lord. Amen.

## Passages for Further Study

6:14-29
8:27-38
10:32-45

## Questions for Consideration:

a) What does Mark's perspective on Christ's death teach us about the place of suffering in the Christian life?
b) What light do Mark's insights about suffering shed upon the mission of the church in the world?
c) To which groups or types of person do you think Mark's understanding of the Cross would be particularly relevant?

# 5
# THE DEATH OF JESUS
# Luke 23:44-49

"It was now about the sixth hour, and darkness came over the whole land until the ninth hour, for the sun stopped shining. And the curtain of the temple was torn in two. Jesus called out with a loud voice, 'Father, into your hands I commit my spirit.' When he had said this, he breathed his last.

The centurion, seeing what had happened, praised God and said, 'Surely this was a righteous man.' When all the people who had gathered to witness this sight saw what took place, they beat their breasts and went away. But all those who knew him, including the women who had followed him from Galilee, stood at a distance, watching these things."

## LUKE

In the previous two chapters we have pictured ourselves standing outside a stately home and looking in to gain as much idea of its shape and contents as possible. Matthew and Mark provided us with such windows—vantage points from which to understand different parts of the suffering and death of Jesus Christ which they wished us to see.

To look through any of Luke's windows is like examining a mural painting. During a visit to Belgium, I went to the site of the Battle of Waterloo. In one of the buildings there, one pays to stand on a central platform and, all around the walls, there is a panoramic presentation of the battle itself. It is a mural full of action, color, and human interest. Luke's Gospel is just like that. It is a panoramic presentation of the story of Jesus, with lots of people milling about as the drama unfolds. Each window gives you access to a different part of the drama.

## BACKDROP

It is the background of the story which first commands attention, however. Luke is showing us a very wide canvas. Whereas Mark begins his story with John the Baptist, and Matthew goes back to Abraham, Luke prefers to begin with Adam. He refers his story to the entire human race. And, at the other end, while Matthew and Mark finish with the Resurrection, Luke goes on to the Ascension of Jesus, thus tying his story to all God's future dealings with the world through Christ. It is clear that Luke wishes to place the ministry of Jesus against the widest possible background.

Yet this wide backdrop places the drama firmly in the world and its affairs. At the beginning, in the dedication of his Gospel, Luke claims to have gathered his evidence from eyewitnesses. He is vouching for the historicity of what he describes. And it is Luke who tells of the vision of angels appearing to the shepherds at the birth of Jesus with a message of peace on earth. The occasion is a specific one in

# The Death of Jesus—Luke

time and place: its benefit is to be for all. This impression that the events he describes are an important part of world affairs is strengthened by his telling us that Caesar Augustus was Emperor at the time of the birth of Jesus, and Quirinius was governor of Syria. And he dates the beginning of Jesus' ministry in the fifteenth year of the reign of Tiberius Caesar, when Pontius Pilate was Roman governor and Herod, Philip, and Lysanias were tetrarchs.

Luke wants us to know that the story of Jesus both took place in a specific historical setting and yet has a significance for all human history. So when the faithful old man, Simeon, takes the baby Jesus in his arms and says the beautiful words of what we know as the *Nunc Dimittis,* he includes the prophecy that this child will be "a light for revelation to the Gentiles and for glory of your people Israel" (2:32). Luke agrees with Matthew and Mark in quoting a prophecy of Isaiah to explain the work of John the Baptist as "a voice of one calling in the desert" (3:4). But only Luke carries on the quotation to include the prophecy, "Every valley shall be filled in, every mountain and hill made low . . . and all mankind will see God's salvation" (3:5-6).

So it is not altogether surprising to discover that, in the Passion story, Luke includes a second trial before Pilate, and gives an account of the trial before Herod. He has already recorded a message from Jesus to Herod and his soldiers. But, what is more, Luke adds darkly, "That day Herod and Pilate became friends—before this they had been enemies" (23:12). The Roman and the Jew, each a realistic political leader, formed an alliance which had no room for the religious idealist, Jesus.

So Luke's first window on the Passion is something of a paradox. He plants the action firmly within the boundaries of time and space, and identifies the people and places involved. Yet the net result shows that the people who mattered all rejected Jesus—Pilate (reluctantly), Herod (mockingly), the chief priests and scribes (vehemently). The way of the Cross is apparently incompatible with the realities of government and political compromise.

Incompatible, yet not irrelevant. The political leaders of his time rejected Jesus, yet, by the end of the Gospel, Luke records the command of the risen Christ to preach his name to all the nations. The forces of law and order put him to death by an exercise of their power, but the risen Christ promises his followers that when the Spirit comes upon them, they will be "clothed with power from on high" (24:49).

Between them the political and religious hierarchies brought his life to an end; yet Luke's Gospel ends on a note of joy and triumph because the disciples are sure that he is still with them, and that they will be engaged in the continuing growth of God's kingdom in the world—a story begun by Luke in his second book, the Acts of the Apostles, and continued to this day in the history of the church.

The two kingdoms—human political rule and God's rule in Christ—need not be incompatible. Luke intentionally places the Passion within a historical setting to demonstrate that political power is not, of itself, inimical to the power Jesus demonstrated, the power of love. Indeed the qualities he embodied—self-giving for others, ability to set people free, concern for the needy—are precisely qualities which matter greatly to political idealists. But Jesus stood for more than

# The Death of Jesus—Luke

that. He saw God's rule as greater than all political authority, and the demands of love as greater than the requirements of expediency. Above all through Luke's window, Jesus showed that penitence for our failure and acknowledgment of our need for God are the doorway to authentic living. What is more, Jesus stands at the doorway as the One through whom we gain admission. And there is the rub. We do not like to submit. We look for other windows.

## ROGUES' GALLERY

Another of Luke's windows on the Passion shows us the people in the mural, and emphasizes their importance. Luke gives some wonderful pictures of people we remember. He alone tells us about the Samaritan (10:25-37), who ignores eight centuries of hatred between the Jewish people and his own to go to the help of a wounded Jew. Only Luke recalls Jesus' story of the Prodigal Son (15:11-24)—the boy who wastes his income, returns home penniless to ask for work as a servant, and finds his father ready to give a party in honor of his return. It is Luke who describes the Pharisee (18:9-14) saying his prayers in the Temple, so full of his own importance before God; while a tax collector, ashamed of himself, stands at the back with head bowed—but he is the one whom God accepts. Zacchaeus (19:1-9), another tax collector, climbs a tree because he is small and cannot see Jesus go by; but Jesus calls him down and asks him to provide hospitality. Then there is the image of the needy neighbor (11:5-10) who bangs on the door at midnight, asking for food because unexpected visitors have arrived; and the widow who goes on pestering a judge till he hears her case (18:1-8).

What a motley crowd the people of Luke's Gospel are! Luke seems to have selected a rogues' gallery for his Gospel. Many of them are people with whom we would not choose to mix. Yet Luke champions their right to be included in the story of Jesus by giving one of their representatives a place of enormous honor.

At the heart of the Passion story Luke, like Matthew and Mark, mentions thieves who died on crosses beside Jesus. But only Luke tells how one of them, admitting that his punishment is deserved, then calls out, "Jesus, remember me when you come into your kingdom." He receives the reply, "I tell you the truth, today you will be with me in paradise" (23:42-43). The first person into the kingdom is a penitent criminal.

And this criminal is there to represent all the rest; the despised Samaritan, the good-for-nothing son, the traitor and cheat—and all the others whom society naturally rejects. It is typical of Luke to tell us that the convicted thief takes the first place in the kingdom of God.

Yet through the same window we can see more than outcasts. Luke is determined to include all kinds of underprivileged people. He records Jesus' promises to the poor, the hungry, and the mourner (6:20-21). He highlights the place of women, mentioning thirteen women who do not appear in any of the other Gospels. He shows concern for children, stressing in three cases that they are the only child of the family. Even the Romans, not a very popular nation with the first-century Jews who formed the nucleus of the early Chris-

# The Death of Jesus—Luke

tian church, are shown in a good light, as are tax collectors and Pharisees. Pilate, the Roman governor, is described as presenting a favorable view of Jesus on four separate occasions (23:4, 14, 15, 20). The unlovable, the underprivileged, the despised, and the weak seem far to outnumber the rest in Jesus' priority list. He goes out of his way to answer positively the question, "Do people matter?"

"Do people matter?" That question has a familiar ring about it! As multinational corporations grow in power, international political units are set up, moving the center of decision making further from us, and economic considerations increasingly dominate the scene, we might be forgiven for thinking at times that we do not matter. We feel more like numbers than people, like counters to be moved about on a board rather than persons to be known and understood. For Luke, Christ stands in history as a reminder that in God's world persons do matter. They have a dignity of their own—at family, work, and national levels. Against our natural tendency to assess a person's value by status, ability, or possessions, Luke underlines the intrinsic worth of every human being as a creature of God. So the dying criminal is welcomed, admitting his need of Christ's help and trusting his life into Christ's hands.

Luke has planted the Cross firmly in the marketplace of life. He insists that all who wish to be followers of Jesus can follow. But if they do put their lives into his hands, they will need to give evidence of it in the quality of the lives they lead. False claims to discipleship are soon exposed as sham under the pressures of everyday life. How can anyone survive the test?

Luke says that one way to survive is through prayer, which was one of the disciplines of Jesus' ministry. In Luke's Gospel there are seven accounts of Jesus at prayer which are found nowhere else. And the record reaches its climax with the story of the Cross. As they describe the death of Jesus, Matthew, Mark, and Luke each say that he gave a loud cry; only Luke reveals the content of that cry, "Father, into your hands I commit my spirit!" (23:46). Even at the last he was praying, committing his life wholly into the care of God.

There is no special place in the world, set apart for Christian discipleship, where it can be achieved with ease. It has to be lived out in the same noisy, challenging, demanding world shared by everyone else. There are no special individuals either, chosen because of their superior moral qualities to belong to God's people. There are only people like you and me, whose only qualification is that we know we need God's hand controlling our lives. And what a varied group we are! But we share in common the experience of prayer—that link with the never-ending love of God, which can sustain us in our discipleship, as it did Jesus in his ministry, and in his dying. Luke's mural has reached its end—and its new beginning.

## A Prayer:

We thank you, O God, that the Passion of Jesus took place in the open, where people might see the extent of your love and care. May our discipleship be lived openly, too, sustained by your love. Amen.

# The Death of Jesus—Luke

## Passages for Further Study:

10:25-37
15:11-24
19:1-9

## Questions for Consideration:

a) How important is Luke's emphasis on God's love for every person through Jesus' death?
b) What difference does it make to the mission of the church that Luke puts such emphasis on the outcasts of society?
c) To which groups or types of persons do you think Luke's understanding of the Cross would be particularly relevant today?

# 6
# THE DEATH OF JESUS
## John 19:28-37

"Later, knowing that all was now completed, and so that the Scripture would be fulfilled, Jesus said, 'I am thirsty.' A jar of wine vinegar was there, so they soaked a sponge in it, put the sponge on a stalk of the hyssop plant, and lifted it to Jesus' lips. When he had received the drink, Jesus said, 'It is finished.' With that, he bowed his head and gave up his spirit.

Now it was the day of Preparation, and the next day was to be a special Sabbath. Because the Jews did not want the bodies left on the crosses during the Sabbath, they asked Pilate to have the legs broken and the bodies taken down. The soldiers therefore came and broke the legs of the first man who had been crucified with Jesus, and then those of the other. But when they came to Jesus and found that he was already dead, they did not break his legs. Instead, one of the soldiers pierced Jesus' side with a spear, bringing a sudden flow of blood and water. The man who saw it has given testimony, and his testimony is true. He knows that he tells the truth, and he testifies so that you also may believe. These things happened so that the scripture would be fulfilled: 'Not one of his bones will be broken,' and, as another scripture says, 'They will look on the one they have pierced.'"

## JOHN

Many years ago, I was shown a remarkable work of art. It consisted of all the words of John's Gospel, written in a minute hand. It was not in straight lines, however, but in a curiously circular outline, working into the center. I began by reading the words, turning the page round as I did so. It was some time before I stopped reading, looked at the page as a whole, and discovered that the words were arranged to give the outline of a face, plainly intended to be the face of Jesus Christ. The face needed the words, because the onlooker could not see a face without them. Yet the words needed the face, too, to give life and shape to their meaning.

As we look through the windows on the Passion provided for us by John's Gospel, we have to follow a similar process to that which I discovered in looking at that work of art. All John's windows focus attention on the one portrait of Jesus Christ. Different windows highlight different aspects of the picture, but it is essentially the same portrait throughout. Sometimes we need to look at the detail, provided by John's words, and sometimes we have to stand back and study the overall effect.

## MANY COLORS

The first window focuses attention on the richness of the colors used for John's portrait. He is full of the grandeur of his subject. He is determined to explore big themes about Jesus. In the first fourteen verses alone he writes of Jesus

# The Death of Jesus—John

Christ as the source of life, the giver of light, the embodiment of grace and truth, and the revealer of God's glory. The verbal picture he paints uses color after color, each as rich as the next, to outline the main features of the ministry of Christ. John seems to know that his canvas is not really big enough for the subject, nor his range of color bold enough to make the impression upon us which the subject deserves.

John does not begin his Gospel with a genealogy or a story, as the other Gospel writers do. He begins with God. But he also speaks of another being alongside God, whom he calls "the Word." "In the beginning was the Word, and the Word was with God, and the Word was God. He was with God in the beginning. Through him all things were made; without him nothing was made that has been made" (1:1-3).

So far so good. The idea of God's Word is a familiar Old Testament theme. In the account of creation given in Genesis, God says, "Let there be light" (Gen. 1:3), "and there was light." God's Word has creative power. Also in the Old Testament, God's Word is given to the prophets so that the people might know God's will. God's Word has revealing power.

But John is saying something more than this. Certainly God's Word creates and reveals. But now we see this Word not simply as one of God's characteristics or attitudes. The Word in John's Gospel is God and yet is also with God. We are now thinking not so much about an activity of God but about an agent of God. And because he is the agent of creation and revelation, John now says, "In him was life, and that life was the light of men" (1:4). Creation gives life; revelation gives light; and the Word who is with God is the bringer of both.

No wonder John's canvas is not big enough or his colors

rich enough to do justice to his subject! But he yet has a still bigger shock in store for us. This Word, present with God before creation, the agent of life and light, has lived on earth among us! John writes prosaically, "The Word became flesh and made his dwelling among us" (1:14). John must be joking! God's agent of creation and revelation in human form? Precisely, says John, the Word became flesh and for a while lived among us. "We have seen his glory, the glory of the One and Only, who came from the Father, full of grace and truth" (1:14). Then, lest we still have not grasped it, he adds later, "Grace and truth came through Jesus Christ" (1:17). God's creative revealing Word shares our life as Jesus Christ. As one commentator puts it, "The deeds and words of Jesus are the deeds and words of God; if this be not true the book is blasphemous."

At times we may fear that the picture which we see through this window will turn out to be an impressionistic painting which we cannot explain. Yet the message is clear.

First and obviously, John is telling us something about Jesus Christ himself. He is saying that the only way to make sense of what the disciples experienced of him was to accept that this was the unique Son of God whose existence did not begin with physical birth in first-century Palestine, but somehow pre-dated the universe itself.

We are familiar with this in our assessment of people today. Which of us would wish to suggest that the great violinist Yehudi Menuhin should spend his days playing a fiddle in some country club; or that Winston Churchill should have limited himself to local government politics; or that Chris Evert would have been better off to play tennis only for a local

# The Death of Jesus—John 53

business team? We sense, from what we know and desire of such people, that they are world-size. Any other context for their activities would be narrowing and insulting.

This is why John's Gospel is full of big themes. He wishes us to know that the characteristics of Jesus Christ are meant to be the foundation of all truly human living. The quality of his love for others, the way he set people free from that which imprisoned them, his perception of the presence of God in all of life, his concern for inward purity, are seen as the basis for truly personal fulfillment in any age and place. His size fills eternity.

This is why this Gospel portrays Jesus as the embodiment of life, light, grace, truth, and glory. This, too, is why John recalls the great "I am" sayings of Jesus. "I am the light of the world" (8:12), "I am the way and the truth and the life" (14:6), "I am the gate for the sheep" (10:7), "I am the true vine, and my Father is the gardener" (15:1), "I am the vine; you are the branches" (15:5). At every turn John is assuring us that those qualities which we recognize to be at the very heart of life at its best were perfectly possessed and demonstrated by Jesus Christ. He is the axis around whom the created world is meant to revolve: human and divine life in perfect harmony.

We see the Passion through this window. It is almost natural to read in this Gospel the words, "For God so loved the world that he gave his one and only Son, that whoever believes in him shall not perish but have eternal life" (3:16) and "But I, when I am lifted up from the earth, will draw all (persons) to myself" (12:32). In each case the context makes it plain that, although persons have potential for a fully satisfying human life, what they experience in their own power is anything but that. The alternatives of good and evil, light and darkness, life and death are constantly present. We ourselves are shown as naturally choosing or being overcome by evil, darkness, and death. In this situation John portrays Jesus Christ as the one who is not overcome and does not choose the wrong way.

The sign that all this is true is his death. Jesus uses the picture from the Old Testament story of Moses lifting up a brass serpent in the wilderness so that all who had been bitten by serpents might look on it and be healed. He says that he is to be "lifted up" from the earth—a reference to his death on the Cross—to draw everyone to him. The big themes of John's Gospel are not simply to thrill and stretch our imagination. They are to show us that only the person at the center of the Gospel has the power to lift us out of darkness, evil, and death; and that he will do so if we put our trust in him.

## EARTH TONES

The second window gives us a perspective in stark contrast to these lofty themes. It emphasizes the earthiness of the ministry of Jesus. After all, the Word did become flesh. John also records Jesus' first miracle as taking place at a wedding in Cana of Galilee (2:1-11). There is, too, an earthy realism about the way Jesus measures the devotion of a shepherd to his job by his willingness to lay down his life for his sheep (10:7-18). And John alone describes Jesus' example in washing and drying the feet of his surprised disciples (13:1-17). John's

## The Death of Jesus—John

large themes stimulate the imagination: but he also ensures that they are earthed to the realities of life in the world. Religious leaders refuse to accept the truth Jesus brings (8:12-47). He is maligned for bringing light to a blind man by healing him (9:13-34). He talks of doing the will of God, but the crowd seek to stone him (8:48-59). In the house of the high priest he is struck on the face by an officer of the guard (18:22); while outside his disciple, Peter, is denying that he ever followed Jesus (18:15-18, 25-27). He walks a very difficult and painful road to Jerusalem. As well as the lofty themes, it is a very earthy Christ we meet in John's Gospel.

This directs us straight to the Passion. In a quite literally earthy analogy, Jesus speaks of his forthcoming death in horticultural terms: "I tell you the truth, unless a kernel of wheat falls to the ground and dies, it remains only a single seed. But if it dies, it produces many seeds" (12:24).

Just as the seeds go into the ground and are left desolate and alone, so it is going to be for him. As there is no fruit without planting, so there will be no establishing of God's kingdom without the death of Jesus.

This extremely somber and earthy element in the Gospel is not simply a balance for the exciting themes. It has a note of harsh reality about it. Again and again the setting is the plight of people without Christ. We are seen as being in darkness, likely to perish, under God's wrath. Jesus is seen as the one who can deal with such a situation. He is the embodiment of the creative and revealing Word; he is the way, truth, life, the light, the shepherd, the door. But he is so for us because his life shows us what we might be and his death provides the way for us to be it. He not only dies in place of

Barabbas, the robber. He dies in place of us all. Only John records the great cry from the Cross, "It is finished" (19:30). From the Cross the truth is declared, the light shines, the way is revealed, the door is opened, the shepherd gives his life for the sheep, and life is made available. The seed dies that the fruit may come.

## BELIEVE AND RECEIVE

Here we move to our third window in John, and solve a problem in perspective which is raised by the other two windows. The Word becomes flesh because God loves the world. The manifesto is declared because Greeks, representing the non-Jewish world, come to Jesus (12:20-23). Do the greatness of the themes and the breadth of the offer mean that all persons automatically benefit? Our third window takes us back to the beginning for an answer to that question. "He came to that which was his own, but his own did not receive him" (1:11). The element of human choice figures prominently in John's presentation. Indeed, at the end of the Gospel, he declares his purpose: "But these (things) are written that you may believe that Jesus is the Christ, the Son of God, and that by believing you may have life in his name" (20:31). One scholar has suggested that the purpose of the Gospel of John is to answer the question, "What must I do to be saved?" In many ways it is a very individual Gospel. It both isolates the individuality of Jesus by recording large amounts of his teaching and concentrating on the 'I am' sayings, and also isolates the reader by facing him or her with the chal-

# The Death of Jesus—John

lenge to believe. Twice in Chapter 1, those who are interested are told, "Come and you will see" (1:39, 46). It is not written to stimulate our speculation about the world, or about people, or about God. It is written to face us with the challenge to believe and receive; to believe that Jesus is the Christ, God's chosen one for the world, and to receive eternal life.

"These (things) are written that you may believe that Jesus is the Christ, the Son of God." This is the good news which all the Gospels and the Passion of Christ declare: "and that by believing you may have life in his name."

## A Prayer:

O God, we thank you for the good news in the Gospels of your love for us in Christ, shown supremely in his Passion. Help us to perceive your presence behind the words, and in your presence to choose the light; through Jesus Christ, our Lord. Amen.

## Passages for Further Study:

2:1-11
9:13-34
12:20-23

## Questions for Consideration:

a) What do you learn about the meaning of Christ's death from John's teaching about who Jesus was (e.g., the Word of Creation)?
b) How do John's insights on Jesus' humanity help us to face the big issues of the day in the light of the gospel?
c) To which groups or types of person do you think that John's understanding of the Cross (e.g., believe and receive) would be particularly relevant today?

# GO THROUGH YOUR WINDOW

How are we to respond to the variety of options provided for us in the Gospels, and across the whole New Testament concerning the death of Jesus?

I think we answer that question best by not regarding them as options. Earlier reference to the Jupiter Symphony again becomes instructive. When we first hear a piece of music, we are struck by particular things about it. We may find that the theme is a haunting one. Or we may be struck by the contribution from the strings or the brass. It may simply be the contribution of one instrument—violin, piano, oboe, or even cymbals! We can be sure that if it is a piece of music with high quality, the next time we listen to it there will be something else which impresses us. This new impression will be in part because of the richness of the music, in part because we are now already more familiar with it, and in part because our particular mood, need, context, and attitude will be different from what it was when last we listened.

All this is true about our reading or hearing the story of the death of Jesus, too. Sometimes we need to learn, or be reminded, that it is love which lies at the heart of life, and that God's supreme act of love in Christ's death is the demonstration of it. Sometimes, when we are despondent about our worth, we need to hear that God planned our liberation from despair with such patience and care. At other times we have to discover that although we have done wrong, thought wrong, been wrong, there is one who has "stood in for us" in our guilt, and invites us now to "stand in for him" in the world. So the story goes on and on, interlinking and interlocking with our story as it variously develops. What it is, and who and where we are, all form an essential part of the experience of looking through the various windows onto the Passion.

There is a second point, however, which in some ways qualifies the first. Each of us is temperamentally different from everyone else. In temperament we cannot be other than we are, and this shapes our approach to matters small and large, from what we choose to wear, to whom we choose as life's partner. It would be odd if this did not influence our attitude to the Cross also. Some of us will always find one insight or interpretation more meaningful than the others and wonder why everyone else cannot see its importance as clearly as we do! That should not worry us, so long as we are being as open as we can to all the rest. The man or woman who listens to a Mozart concerto but is actually concentrating only on what the oboe contributes may not be getting the best out of the concert!

There is a third conclusion, without which the meaning of the other two may be lost. In the end, our response to the death of Jesus is not like looking through a window or listening to a piece of music. Both can be very passive experiences. By contrast, responding to the death of Jesus is essentially active. Certainly we are on the receiving end of God's grace. Our salvation is fundamentally dependent upon God's initiative through Jesus Christ. We did not initiate the saving work of Christ on which we depend. We do not deserve any of the grace which God lavishes upon us. Salvation by grace through faith underlines strongly our desperate need of God's gracious initiative toward us. Nevertheless, our reception of this grace is not passive, if that were taken to mean that we simply accept. Faith, in the New Testament, means more than believing. It carries strong implications of commitment and trust. The point of our sacraments of baptism and Holy Communion is that we willingly identify ourselves by faith with his death and resurrection. We submit to being buried and raised with Christ, not only as the beginning of faith but also as a daily experience of dying to all that Christ died to and rising to all that he rose to. It means being actively committed to all that following Christ involves in discipleship. This means that we begin with the understanding of Christ's death that best meets our need and temperament. It also means that we are committed to the broadening of our understanding and of our experience in relation to Christ's death. Whichever window we begin with or find most congenial, the challenge of discipleship to Jesus is a challenge to look through every window possible, to listen to every bit of the music available, and to live with all our might according to the implications of all that we have seen and heard. This book has sought to point to the windows and release the music. The rest remains with God's Spirit and the disciples' response.